The Art and Artist's
Quotation Book

The
Art and Artist's
Quotation Book

A Literary Companion

Edited by
HELEN HALE

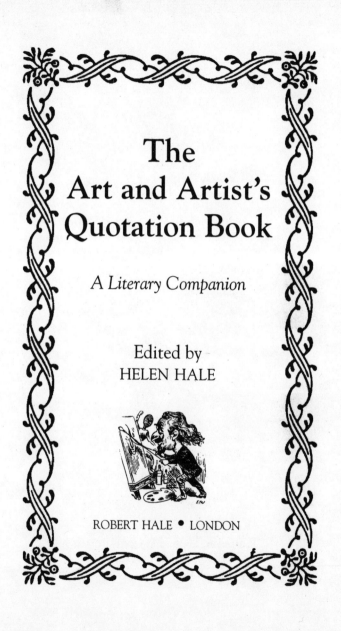

ROBERT HALE • LONDON

Robert Hale Limited
Clerkenwell House
Clerkenwell Green
London EC1R 0HT

Printed and bound in Great Britain
by WBC Book Manufacturers Ltd,
Bridgend, Mid-Glamorgan

Preface

'Some books are to be tasted, others to be swallowed, and some few to be chewed and digested; that is, some books are to be read only in parts; others to be read but not curiously; some few to be read wholly, and with diligence and attention.'

Thus wrote the other *Francis Bacon, Viscount St Albans, in about 1600. Books of quotations would generally fall into the first category, but when it comes to Art, however, there are as many conflicting ideas as there are shades of colour; the prudent reader should be prepared therefore for the occasional chewy and unpalatable morsel.*

My search for words of wisdom and wit from the masters has, of course, been fascinating, and could have continued indefinitely had it not been for the limitations of time and space. Consequently this small collection is presented in what Marcel Duchamp would call 'a final state of incompletion'.

The greatest difficulty has, predictably, been that of selection and my choice has been weighted on the side of first-hand information, for who should know better than the artist? Some of the advice I have encountered has had to be abandoned on the grounds of impracticability and frivolity – notably that of Walter Sickert who urged every aspiring young painter to take a large studio and 'If you can't afford to take one, take two!' However, everyone who has ever had the temerity, or perhaps foolhardiness, to embark on their own work of art should find some food for thought.

Art was dead in 1911, according to Rodin, but fortunately nobody else seems to have noticed, least of all artists who tend in any case to pursue, regardless, their own creative urges and obsessions; indeed, from past to present times some have persisted in their work to the detriment of their health and sanity, endured public ridicule or total neglect, and lived and died in poverty. The reason for such dedication to their art is, as it has always been, as much of a mystery as life itself. One might say that it is the unreasonable in pursuit of the indefinable.

The subject of Art, nevertheless, is too important to be left entirely to artists. My task would certainly have been less time-consuming since they do not, on the whole, like to write about it, but since art historians, writers and critics do, and have expressed themselves at considerable length, they must also be included.

In spite of all the words, though, the essential mystery of Art remains: there are no rules, no ultimate definition of what it is, or is not. There is no answer. 'In that case,' in the last recorded words of Gertude Stein, 'what is the question?'

HELEN HALE

Painting . . . was first invented, saith Patricius, *ex amoris beneficio*, for love's sake. For when the daughter of Dibutades the Dicyonian was to take leave of her sweetheart now going to wars, *ut desiderio ejus minus tabesceret*, to comfort herself in his absence, she took his picture with coal upon a wall, as the candle gave the shadow, which her father admiring perfected afterwards, and it was the first picture by report that ever was made.

ROBERT BURTON (1577–1640)
Anatomy of Melancholy

'I've taken up art.'
'Why?'
'Well, since the opposite of art is insensibility, a life that is mute, formless, unexpressed, emptily repetitive, vacuous routine with failure of creativity and . . .'
'Good grief! Chuck me some clay!'

HARGREAVES
Hayseeds cartoon strip

Art is a passion or it is nothing.

ROGER FRY (1866–1934)
Vision and Design

The artist is not a special kind of man, but every man is a special kind of artist.

ANANDA COOMRASWAMY (1877–1947)
Transformation of Nature in Art

When Millais said 'Art', he meant British art. And when he said 'British Art' he meant the painting of John Everett Millais. And we loved him so greatly that nobody so much as squeaked.

WALTER SICKERT (1860–1942)
A Free House!

Every art changes inevitably in its manifestations as its creators develop, but less than one might think: it always keeps its simple, noble function, indispensable to man, which is to *communicate*.

KAREL KUPKA
Dawn of Art, 1965

Books are the true means of acquiring talent, for if one does not read one remains ignorant, and ignorance can never produce true painters.

FRANCESCO ALBANI (1578–1660)
Treatise on Painting

Ah, sir, as to the artist in England! I have often thought it would solve a great many problems if English painters were born blind.

WYNDHAM LEWIS (1882–1957)

Whistler declared that his health had been ruined 'by living in the midst of English pictures'.

of James Abbot McNeill Whistler (1834–1903)

Does he paint? he fain would write a poem. Does he
write? he fain would paint a picture.
ROBERT BROWNING (1812–89)
One Word More

Art today is a new kind of instrument, an instrument for
modifying consciousness and organizing new modes of
sensibility . . . Artists have had to become self-conscious
aestheticians: continually challenging their means, their
materials and methods.
SUSAN SONTAG (born 1933)
Against Interpretation

For painters, poets and builders have very high flights,
but they must be kept down.
> SARAH, FIRST DUCHESS OF MARLBOROUGH
> (1660–1744)
> letter to the Duchess of Bedford
> 1734

The function of Art is to disturb. Science reassures.
> GEORGES BRAQUE (1882–1963)
> *Cahier*
> 1948

I think my work is to do with upsetting something. Quite
definitely.
> BRIDGET RILEY (born 1931)
> *The Times Magazine*, March 1994

Every creative act involves . . . a new innocence of perception, liberated from the cataract of accepted belief.
> ARTHUR KOESTLER (1905–83)
> *The Sleepwalkers*

Shall I tell you what I think are the two qualities of a
work of art? First, it must be indescribable, and, second,
it must be inimitable.
> AUGUSTE RENOIR (1841–1914)
> interview with Walter Pach
> *Scribner's Magazine*, May 1912

I am for an art that takes its forms from the lines of life itself, that twists and extends and accumulates and spits and drips and is heavy and coarse and blunt and sweet and stupid as life itself.

> CLAES OLDENBURG (born 1929)
> exhibition catalogue, 1961

Abstract art is the result of an attempt to make pictures more real, an attempt to come nearer to the essence of painting.

> ROGER HILTON (1911–75)
> Lawrence Alloway, *Nine Abstract Artists*

What is one to think of those fools who tell one that the artist is always subordinate to nature? Art is a harmony parallel with nature.

> PAUL CÉZANNE (1839–1906)
> to Joachim Gasquet in 1897

All art is an abstraction to some degree.

> HENRY MOORE (1898–1986)
> *Unit One*
> edited by Herbert Read

The most sensible men I know (taken as a class) are painters; that is, they are the most lively observers of what passes in the world about them, and the closest observers of what passes in their own minds. From their profession they in general mix more with the world than authors; and if they have not the same fund of acquired knowledge, are obliged to rely more on individual sagacity. I might mention the names of Opie, Fuseli, Northcote, as persons distinguished for striking description and acquaintance with the subtle traits of character. Painters in ordinary society, or in obscure situations where their value is not known, and they are treated with neglect and indifference, have sometimes a forward self-sufficiency of manner; but this is not so much their fault as that of others. Perhaps their want of regular education may also be in fault in such cases. Richardson, who is very tenacious of the respect in which the profession ought to be held, tells a story of Michael Angelo, that after a quarrel between him and Pope Julius II 'upon account of a slight the artist conceived the Pontiff had put upon him, Michael Angelo was introduced by a bishop, who, thinking to serve the artist by it, made it an argument that the Pope should be reconciled to him, because men of his profession were commonly ignorant, and of no consequence otherwise: his holiness, enraged at the bishop, struck him with his staff, and told him, it was he that was the blockhead, and affronted the man himself would not offend; the prelate was driven out of the chamber, and Michael Angelo had the Pope's benediction accompanied with presents.'

WILLIAM HAZLITT (1778–1830)
Table Talk

Painting isn't so difficult when you don't know . . . But when you do . . . it's quite a different matter!
 EDGAR DEGAS (1834–1917)
 from *Degas Dance Drawing* by Paul Valéry

Sir William Nicholson – a fine artist – told me often that it was easy to put on the paint if you knew where to put it.

SIR ALFRED MUNNINGS (1878–1959)
An Artist's Life

Do not imagine that Art is something which is designed to give gentle uplift and self-confidence. Art is not a *brassière*. At least, not in the English sense. But do not forget that *brassière* is the French for life-jacket.

JULIAN BARNES (born 1946)
Flaubert's Parrot

A certain strangeness, something of the blossoming of the aloe, is indeed an element in all true works of art: that they shall excite or surprise us is indispensable. But that they shall give pleasure and exert a charm over us is indispensable too; and this strangeness must be sweet also – a lively strangeness.

WALTER PATER (1839–94)
The Renaissance

Life is very nice, but it lacks form. It's the aim of art to give it some.

JEAN ANOUILH (born 1910)
The Rehearsal
1950

The learned understand the theory of art, the unlearned its pleasure.

> QUINTILIAN (AD c. 35–100)
> *De Institutione Oratoria*

To me Art's subject is the human clay,
And landscape but a background to a torso;
All Cézanne's apples I would give away
For one small Goya or a Daumier.

> W.H. AUDEN (1907–73)
> *Letter to Lord Byron III*

I have been fortunate enough to lead, unlike Chagall, an uneventful life.

> GIORGIO MORANDI (1890–1964)
> Edouard Roditi, *Dialogues*: Conversations with European Artists at Mid-Century
> 1958

One must always be careful not to let one's work be covered with moss.

> MARC CHAGALL (1887–1985)

What a miserable sad thing it is to be fit for painting *only* and nothing else.

> FORD MADOX BROWN (1821–93)
> diary, 31 August 1855

Art itself has become an extraordinary thing – the activity of peculiar people – people who become more and more peculiar as their activity becomes more and more extraordinary.

ERIC GILL (1882–1940)
Art

Painters are subject to trembling of the joints, blackness of the teeth, discoloured complexion, melancholy, and loss of the sense of smell.

BERNARDINO RAMAZZINI (1633–1714)
De Morbis Artificium Diatriba, 1700

Patronage and sponsorship of the arts are, in their purest forms, a kind of emotional stock with a high yield cultural return . . . . In this new guise of enlightened self-interest, it has become 'the business of business' to support this cultural imperative.

MARJORY JACOBSON
Art and Business: New Strategies for Corporate Collecting

[or, to put it another way:]

Art is cultural insurance. Take out a policy now.

THEO CROSBY (1925–94)
How to Play the Environment Game

Like all great art the moment you are looking at it there is nothing else, and nothing else can be done. That is the sense in which art is like a love affair.

> NORMAN ROSENTHAL (born 1944)
> *Royal Academy Magazine*, 1993

Right now architecture and sculpture are calling to each other, and calling for a response that's intelligent, not for more ghastly lumps of sculpture . . . which have no sense of scale and are just plonked down in public places.

> SIR ANTHONY CARO (born 1924)
> in an interview with Tim Marlow for *Tate: The Art Magazine*, 1994

Architecture is the art of how to waste space.

> PHILIP JOHNSON (born 1906)
> *The New York Times*, 1964

In my experience, if you have to keep the lavatory door shut by extending your left leg, it's modern architecture.

> NANCY BANKS-SMITH
> *The Guardian*, 1979

I had thought Bauhaus was the German for kennel.

> STEPHANIE LEWIS
> *The Times*
> 26 February 1994

No language worth the name can forget the past. We see all around us the dire results of the modernists' attempt to ignore everything that went before. A new language will grow out of older ones and be in sympathy . . .
> *Art and Architecture Manifesto*
> 1989

When you pay high for the priceless, you're getting it cheap.
> LORD DUVEEN OF MILLBANK (1869–1939)

I have the loftiest idea, and the most passionate one, of art. Much too lofty to agree to subject it to anything. Much too passionate to want to divorce it from anything.
> ALBERT CAMUS (1913–61)
> *Notebooks, 1942–51*

Artists who approach perfection do not have many ideas.
> ODILON REDON (1840–1916)
> *To Myself: Journal*

However bad an artist, his work is his life; the worse it is the greater his vanity.
> SIR ALFRED MUNNINGS (1878–1959)
> *An Artist's Life*

Only bad painters enjoy painting.
> CECIL COLLINS (born 1908)
> from the Tate Gallery exhibition catalogue, 1989

If I didn't start painting, I would have raised chickens.
>GRANDMA MOSES (née Anna Mary Robertson;
>1860–1961)
>*My Life's History*

The canvas upon which the artist paints is the spectator's mind.
>KAKUZO OKAKURA (1862–1913)
>*The Book of Tea*

Art is both creation and recreation. Of the two ideas, I think art as recreation or as sheer play of the human spirit is more important.
>LIN YUTANG (1895–1976)
>*The Importance of Living*

The creative process? . . . You just say to yourself I feel like doing so and so, I think it's that simple.
>LOUISE NEVELSON (1899–1988)

Just as Leonardo da Vinci studied human anatomy and dissected corpses, so I try to dissect souls.
>EDVARD MUNCH (1863–1944)

These are very good, but I prefer my own.
>GWEN JOHN (1876–1939)
>on seeing an exhibition of Cézanne's watercolours as quoted in the Arts Council of Great Britain's catalogue for 'Gwen John: A Retrospective Exhibition'

A man's life *is* his work; his work *is* his life.
JACKSON POLLOCK (1912–56)

In my experience, anyone can paint if he doesn't have to
. . . During my apprentice days I felt encouraged by the
advice of Winston Churchill . . . 'Don't be afraid of the
canvas.' I have now reached the point where the canvas
is afraid of me.
BEATRICE LILLIE (1898–1988)
Every Other Inch a Lady, 1927

I don't advise any one to take it [painting] up as a business proposition, unless they really have talent . . . But I
will say that I have did remarkable for one of my years,
and experience.
GRANDMA MOSES (née Anna Mary Robertson;
1860–1961)
The New York Times, 11 May 1947

I hope always to earn my living by my art without having
ever deviated by even a hair's breadth from my principles,
without having lied to my conscience for a single
moment, without painting even as much as can be covered by a hand only to please anyone or to sell more
easily.
GUSTAVE COURBET (1819–77)
letter to Alfred Bruyas
May, 1854

Work lovingly done is the secret of all order and all happiness.

AUGUSTE RODIN (1840–1917)

To explain away the mystery of a great painting – if such a feat were possible – would be irreparable harm . . . If there is no mystery then there is no 'poetry'.

GEORGES BRAQUE (1882–1963)
to John Richardson
Observer, December 1957

Painting is stronger than I am. It can make me do whatever it wants.

PABLO PICASSO (1881–1973)
a note written in the back of one of his sketchbooks

Now that I know what I want, I don't have to hold on to it quite so much.

LUCIAN FREUD (born 1922)
Private View, Robertson/Russell/Snowdon

Cézanne is the Christopher Columbus of a new continent of form.

CLIVE BELL (1881–1964)
Art

I am always at work, but not in order to arrive at that finish which arouses the admiration of idiots.

PAUL CÉZANNE (1839–1906)
letter to his mother in 1874

I think painting today 'is pure intuition and luck and taking advantage of what happens when you splash the stuff down.'

FRANCIS BACON (1909–92)
exhibition catalogue for Matthew Smith Retrospective, 1953

A little before my Comming to the City, Cavaliero Bernini, Sculptor, Architect, Painter & Poet . . . gave a Publique Opera where in he painted the Seanes, cut the Statues, invented the Engines, composed the Musique, writ the Comedy and built the Theatre all himself.
JOHN EVELYN (1620–1706)
Diary, 1644

Whenever I see Frans Hals I feel like painting, but when I see a Rembrandt I feel like giving up!
MAX LIEBERMANN (1847–1935)

Vasari records that after introducing Michelangelo to Titian, who was then working on a picture of Danaë, Michelangelo said 'that Titian's colouring and his style much pleased him, but that it was a pity that in Venice men did not learn to draw well from the beginning, and that those painters did not pursue a better method in their studies'.
Lives of the Painters, Sculptors, and Architects
1550

A painting requires a little mystery, some vagueness, some fantasy. When you always make your meaning perfectly plain you end up boring people.
EDGAR DEGAS (1834–1917)
Georges Jeanniot, *Memories of Degas*
1933

Speaking to a lawyer about pictures is something like talking to a butcher about humanity.

> JOHN CONSTABLE (1776–1837)
> letter to John Fisher, Bishop of Salisbury
> 17 January, 1824

The one thing that marks the true artist is a clear perception and a firm, bold hand, in distinction from that imperfect mental vision and uncertain touch which give us the feeble pictures and the lumpy statues of the mere artisans on canvas or in stone.

> OLIVE WENDELL HOLMES (1809–94)
> *The Professor at the Breakfast Table*

It was Richepin who said somewhere: 'The love of art means loss of real love.' . . . True, but on the other hand, real love makes you disgusted with art.

> VINCENT VAN GOGH (1853–90)
> letter to his brother, Theo
> March, 1886

Art is a human activity, consisting in this, that one man consciously, by means of certain external signs, hands on to others feelings he has lived through, and that other people are infected by these feelings, and also experience them.

> LEO TOLSTOY (1828–1910)
> *What is Art?* (trans. Aylmer Maude)

A work of art is not a matter of thinking beautiful thoughts or experiencing tender emotions (though those are its raw materials), but of intelligence, skill, taste, proportion, knowledge, discipline and industry; especially discipline.

EVELYN WAUGH (1903–66)
Letters

I begin with an idea and then it becomes something else.

PABLO PICASSO (1881–1973)

In painting, you have to destroy in order to gain . . . you have got to sacrifice something you are quite pleased with in order to get something better. Of course, it's a risk . . . .

GRAHAM SUTHERLAND (1903–80)
Daily Express, 30 November, 1954

8th   scraped & cuttled away at the sky & sea (6 hours)
9th   to work by 12 at the sky. It was all wrong and is
        now worse (6 hours)
10th do. from 10 till ½ past 7 at the sky with scarcely
        any result (7½ hours)
11th do. from 10 till 4, improved it.
        FORD MADOX BROWN (1821–93)
        diary, August 1855

A mature artist is at the same time aware of the futility of
his achievement and of the validity of the pursuit.
        JEAN HÉLION (born 1904)
        Gyorgy Kepes, *The Man-Made Object*

Art is coming face to face with yourself. That's what's
wrong with [Thomas Hart] Benton. He came face to face
with Michelangelo – and he lost.
        JACKSON POLLOCK (1912–56)

I know I shall not live very long . . . If I've painted three
good pictures, then I shall leave gladly with flowers in my
hand and my hair.
        PAULA MODERSOHN-BECKER (1876–1907)
        diary, 26 July 1900

I was very embarrassed when my canvases began to fetch
high prices. I saw myself condemned to a future of nothing but masterpieces.
        HENRI MATISSE (1869–1954)
        interview with Jacques Guenne, 1925

There is nothing harder to learn than painting and nothing which most people take less trouble about learning. An art school is a place where about three people work with feverish energy and everybody else idles to a degree that I should have conceived unattainable by human nature.

G.K. CHESTERTON (1874–1936)
Autobiography

Muscles I know; they are my friends. But I have forgotten their names.

J.A.D. INGRES (1780–1867)
to Edgar Degas
diaries of Daniel Halévy

Here Reynolds is laid, and, to tell you my mind,
He has not left a better or wiser behind:
His pencil was striking, resistless, and grand;
His manners were gentle, complying, and bland;
Still born to improve us in every part,
His pencil our faces, his manners our heart:
To coxcombs averse, yet most civilly steering,
When they judg'd without skill he was still hard of
    hearing:
When they talk'd of their Raphaels, Coreggios, and
    stuff,
He shifted his trumpet, and only took snuff.

OLIVER GOLDSMITH (?1730–74)
Retaliation

He who resolves never to ransack any mind but his own, will be soon reduced, from mere barrenness, to the poorest of all imitations; he will be obliged to imitate himself, and to repeat what he has before often repeated.

SIR JOSHUA REYNOLDS (1723–92)
Discourse
10 December 1774

I certainly do Thank God that I am not like Reynolds.

WILLIAM BLAKE (1757–1827)
Marginalia

ANNOTATIONS TO SIR JOSHUA REYNOLD'S DISCOURSES
This Man was Hired to Depress Art.

This is the Opinion of Will Blake: my proofs of this Opinion are given in the following Notes.

Advice of the Popes who succeeded the Age of Raphael

Degrade first the Arts if you'd Mankind Degrade.
Hire Idiots to Paint with cold light & hot shade:
Give high price for the worst, leave the best in disgrace,
And with Labours of Ignorance fill every place.

Having spent the Vigour of my Youth & Genius under the Opression of Sr Joshua & his Gang of Cunning Hired Knaves Without Employment & as much as could possibly be Without Bread, The Reader must Expect to Read in all my Remarks on these Books Nothing but Indignation & Resentment. While Sr Joshua was rolling in Riches Barry was Poor & Unemploy'd except by his own Energy; Mortimer was call'd a Madman, & only Portrait Painting applauded & rewarded by the Rich &

Great. Reynolds & Gainsborough Blotted & Blurred one against the other & Divided all the English World between them. Fuseli, Indignant, almost hid himself. I am hid.

> WILLIAM BLAKE (1757–1827)
> *Marginalia*

All Artists are Anarchists.

> GEORGE BERNARD SHAW (1856–1950)
> to Augustus John, *c*.1945
> *Chiaroscuro*

Art is long, life short, judgment difficult, opportunity transient. To act is easy, to think is hard; to act according to our thought is troublesome. Every beginning is cheerful; the threshold is the place of expectation.

> JOHANN WOLFGANG VON GOETHE
> (1749–1832)
> *Wilhelm Meister's Apprenticeship*

Art is a half effaced recollection of a higher state from which we have fallen since the time of Eden.

> SAINT HILDEGARDE
> (1098–1179)

As my poor father used to say
 In 1863,
Once people start on all this Art
 Good-bye, moralitee!
And what my father used to say
 Is good enough for me.
 A.P. HERBERT (1890–1971)
 Lines for a Worthy Person

To the Grafton Gallery to look at . . . the Post-Impressionist pictures sent over from Paris . . . The drawing is on the level of that of an untaught child of seven or eight years old, the sense of colour that of a tea-tray painter, the method that of a schoolboy who wipes his fingers on a slate after spitting on them . . . Apart from the frames, the whole collection should not be worth £5, and then only for the pleasure of making a bonfire of them . . . These are not works of art at all, unless throwing a handful of mud against a wall may be called one. They are the works of idleness and impotent stupidity, a pornographic show.
 WILFRID SCAWEN BLUNT (1840–1922)
 My Diaries
 15 November, 1910

Watts, if I could paint, and you could draw, what an artist we should be!
 LORD LEIGHTON (1830–96)
 to G.F. Watts

It is only by drawing often, drawing everything, drawing incessantly, that one fine day you discover to your surprise that you have rendered something in its true character.

> CAMILLE PISSARRO (1830–1903)
> letter to his son, Lucien; translated by Lionel Abel
> 21 May, 1883

The airless studios grow stifling. Kick the door open – the hum of life turns into a roar.

> FELIKS TOPOLSKI (1907–89)
> BBC Third Programme
> 1946

A critic at my house sees some paintings. Greatly perturbed, he asks for my drawings. My drawings? Never! They are my letters, my secrets.

> PAUL GAUGUIN (1848–1903)
> *Intimate Journals*

It does not matter how badly you paint, so long as you don't paint badly like other people.

> GEORGE MOORE (1852–1933)
> *Confessions of a Young Man*
> 1888

As in the fourteen lines of a sonnet, a few strokes of the pencil can hold immensity.

> DAME LAURA KNIGHT (1877–1970)
> *The Magic of a Line*

Subjective artists are one-eyed, but objective artists are blind.

> GEORGES ROUAULT (1871–1958)
> Robert Speaight, 'Homage to Rouault'; *The Dublin Review*, July 1941

His sketches are so crude that his pencil strokes show more force than judgment and seem to have been made by chance.

> GIORGIO VASARI (1511–76)
> of Tintoretto
> *Lives of the Painters, Sculptors, and Architects*

OSCAR WILDE: You know how well known you are in
    England –
EDGAR DEGAS: Fortunately less so than you.
    DANIEL HALÉVY
    diary, 2 January, 1896

The so-called conscientiousness of the majority of
painters is only perfection applied to the *art of boring*.
    EUGÈNE DELACROIX (1796–1863)
    Journal
    1850

Detail is the heart of realism, and the fatty degeneration
of art.
    CLIVE BELL (1881–1964)
    Art

It is to be observed, that *straight lines* vary only in length,
and therefore are least ornamental. That *curv'd lines* as
they can be varied in their degrees of curvature as well as
in their length, begin on that account to be ornamental.
That straight and curv'd lines joined, being a *compound
line*, vary more than curves alone, and so become some-
what more ornamental. That the *waving line*, or line of
beauty, varying still more, being composed of two curves
contrasted, becomes still more ornamental and pleasing
. . . and that the *serpentine line*, or line of grace, by its
waving and winding at the same time different ways,
leads the eye in a pleasing manner along the continuity
of its variety.
    WILLIAM HOGARTH (1697–1764)
    The Analysis of Beauty

Always lines, never forms! But where do they *find* these lines in Nature? For my part I see only forms that are lit up and forms that are not. There is only light and shadow.

> FRANCISCO JOSÉ DE GOYA Y LUCIENTES (1746–1828)
> in a rare conversation about painting
> L. Matheron, *Goya*; Paris, 1858

Matisse has all the worst art-school tricks. Just a dashing hint of anatomy is obtruded; and you will find a line separating the light from the shade. You know what we think of that trick.

> WALTER SICKERT (1860–1942)
> *A Free House!*

Then we went to Matisse's studio He's one of the neo, neo Impressionists, quite interesting and lots of talent but very queer. He does things very much like Pamela's [Fry's 7-year-old daughter].

> ROGER FRY (1866–1934)
> letter to his wife
> 1909

I am now completely Matissiste . . . after studying all his paintings I am quite convinced of his genius.

> ROGER FRY (1866–1934)
> letter to Simon Bussy
> 1911

When I was their age I could draw like Raphael, but it took me a lifetime to learn to draw like them.
PABLO PICASSO (1881–1973)
after studying an exhibition of children's drawings

Stationers' are nice but artists' colourmen's emporia are mysterious museums of delight.
SHENA MACKAY
Writing on the Wall: Women Writers on Women Artists

The drawing of Michelangelo and the colours of Titian.
JACOPO ROBUSTI, called Tintoretto (1518–94)
words written on the walls of his studio

I entreat fresh visions from the painters,
Be lavish with your vermilion to portray the mountains in the spring.
LU XUN (1881–1936)

With all their damned talk of modern painting, I've been forty years discovering that the queen of all colours is black!
PIERRE AUGUSTE RENOIR (1841–1919)
on emerging one day from the Louvre
Ambroise Vollard, *Recollections of a Picture Dealer*

Artists can colour the sky red because they *know* it's blue. The rest of us, who aren't artists, must colour things the way they really are, or people might think we're stupid.
>JULES FEIFFER (born 1929)
>*Crawling Arnold* (1959)

The fundamental *grey* which differentiates the masters, expresses them and is the soul of all colour.
>ODILON REDON (1840–1916)
>*To Myself: Journal*

How lovely yellow is!
>VINCENT VAN GOGH (1853–90)
>letter to his brother, Theo

What a horrible thing yellow is.
>EDGAR DEGAS (1834–1917)
>*Notebooks*, 1858

A visitor to Le Douanier Rousseau's studio heard him announce with satisfaction that he was on to his twenty-second shade of green.

Blue is the male principle, stern and spiritual. Yellow the female principle, gentle, cheerful and sensual. Red is matter, brutal and heavy and always the colour which must be fought and vanquished by the other two.
>FRANZ MARC (1880–1916)
>letter to August Macke

Renoir said once that nothing was so difficult, and at the same time so exciting, to paint, as white on white.

> AMBROISE VOLLARD
> *Recollections of a Picture Dealer*

I make black and white prints because I want to go back to the beginning, and because in prints black and white are absolute: these two colours express the most delicate vibration, the most profound tranquillity, and unlimited profundity.

> SHIKŌ MUNAKATA (1903–75)

Nothing is so difficult as to give life to colour. I have always wanted my colours to sing.

> PAUL DELVAUX (1897–1994)
> to Martin Bailey
> *tate: the art magazine*, 1994

We mustn't forget to look in at Gérard's window. There's a Jongkind there . . . Such a magnificent sky, and it's nothing but white paper!

> AUGUSTE RENOIR (1841–1914)
> to Ambroise Vollard
> *Recollections of a Picture Dealer*

There were apples painted in pale green and bright red on a ground of emerald green leaves. It is all colour. One might say it was a Cézanne.

> MAURICE DENIS (1870–1943)
> on discovering a fragment of a frieze by Tintoretto
> at the Scuola di san Rocco in 1905

He who knows how to appreciate colour relationships, the influence of one colour on another, their contrasts and dissonances, is promised an infinitely diverse imagery.

SONIA DELAUNAY (1885–1979)
Jacques Damase, *Sonia Delaunay: Rhythms and Colours*

Limning is a thing apart from all other painting or drawing, and tendeth not to comon mens vsse, either for furnishing of howsses or any patterns for tapistries, or building, or for any work whatsoeuer, and yet it excelleth all other painting whatsoeuer in sondry points . . . and is for the seruice of noble persons very meet in small voloms in priuat maner for them to haue the portraits and pictures of themselues, their peers or any other . . . .

NICHOLAS HILLYARDE (c. 1547–1619)
A Treatise concerning the Arte of Limning, c. 1600

A PORTRAIT PAINTER
Good Mr. Fortune, A.R.A.,
    Rejoiced in twenty sons,
But even there he failed, they say,
    To get a likeness once.
    G.R. HAMILTON
    from Lucilius

A good form strikes all eyes pleasantly, long before they have any science on the subject; and a beautiful face sets twenty hearts in palpitation, prior to all consideration of the mechanical proportions of the features and head.
    RALPH WALDO EMERSON (1803–82)
    Essays

Painting the faces of this one and that one
In the world I won infinite merit:
For carving out horns for my husband
I laid down the brush and took up the chisel.
    Il Cimiterio Epitafi Giocosi: A satirical epitaph to Artemisia Gentileschi
    GIOVANNI FRANCESCO LOREDANO and PIETRO MICHIELE
    1654
    Germaine Greer, *The Obstacle Race*

Another enemy made!
    JOHN SINGER SARGENT (1856–1925)
    as he sent off a finished portrait

41

Sir Joshua Reynolds (1723–92) described himself as being 'of near equal dignity with His Majesty's rat catcher' because he was paid so little for his portraits and treated with disdain.

> I drew men's faces on my copy-books,
> Scrawled them within the antiphonary's marge,
> Joined legs and arms to the long music-notes,
> Found nose and eyes and chin for A.s and B.s.,
> And made a string of pictures of the world
> Betwixt the ins and outs of verb and noun,
> On the wall, the bench, the door.
> ROBERT BROWNING (1812–92)
> *Fra Lippo Lippi*

To think that I have known Willie since 1902 and have only just recognized that, disguised as an old madame, he kept a brothel in Shanghai!
> SIR GERALD KELLY (1879–1972)
> on seeing Graham Sutherland's Portrait of W. Somerset Maugham

To paint a head from life, to try and seize it as it is, seems as urgent to me as it was urgent to paint a pure square in 1906.
> AVIGDOR ARIKHA (born 1929)
> 'What Modernity?'
> *Modern Painters*: A Quarterly Journal of the Fine Arts, summer 1994

For Heaven's sake put away that jar of cold cream! You know how Monsieur Vuillard puts in everything he sees.

MADAME DE NOAILLES (1876–1933)
to her maid, before sitting to Vuillard for her portrait

Confound the nose, there's no end to it.

THOMAS GAINSBOROUGH (1727–88)
referring to Mrs Sarah Siddon's large nose which is said to have caused him great trouble when painting her portrait in 1785

If you don't know them, it can only be like a travel book.

LUCIAN FREUD (born 1922)
on the artist in relation to the sitter
Lawrence Gowing, *Lucian Freud*

No longer shall I paint interiors, and people reading, and women knitting. I shall paint living people who breathe and feel and suffer and love.

> EDVARD MUNCH (1863–1944)
> in his journal of 1889

Said the Duchess of Alba to Goya,
 'Do some pictures to hang in my foyer':
  So he painted her twice –
  In the nude to look nice,
And then in her clothes to annoy 'er.

> CYRIL BIBBY
> *The Art of the Limerick*

It's really absurd to make an image, like a human image, with paint, today, when you think about it . . . But then all of a sudden, it was even more absurd not to do it.

> WILLEM DE KOONING (born 1904)
> to David Sylvester

Roger Fry is painting me. It is too like me at present, but he is confident he will be able to alter that. Post-Impressionism is at present confined to my lower lip . . . and to my chin.

> E.M. FORSTER (1879–1970)
> letter to Florence Barger
> 24 December, 1911

Cézanne had one hundred and fifteen sittings for a portrait of Ambroise Vollard and then abandoned it with the remark: 'I am not altogether displeased with the shirt-front.'

Someone said to Renoir one day, 'We are trying to get you the portrait of the Duchess of X to do.'

'Oh, don't bother,' he replied hastily. 'I am happy with the first draggle-tail that comes along, provided she has good firm buttocks and breasts.'

> AMBROISE VOLLARD (1867–1939)
> *Recollections of a Picture Dealer*

There are only two styles of portrait painting; the serious and the smirk.

> CHARLES DICKENS (1812–70)
> *Nicholas Nickleby*

Don't listen to the fools who say that pictures of people can be of no consequence, or that painting is dead. There is much to be done.

> R.B. KITAJ (born 1932)
> Preface to the 'Human Clay' exhibition of 1976

At one point I found myself standing before an oil of a horse that I figure was probably a self-portrait judging from the general execution.

> PETER DE VRIES
> *Let Me Count the Ways*
> 1965

I would rather see the portrait of a dog that I know, than all the allegorical paintings they can shew me in the world.

SAMUEL JOHNSON (1709–84)
Johnsonian Miscellanies ed. G.B. Hill (1897)

If my people look as if they're in a dreadful fix, it's because I can't get them out of a technical dilemma.

FRANCIS BACON (1909–1992)
to David Sylvester
Interviews with Francis Bacon

He showed them to be rich; looking at his portraits they understood at last *how* rich they really were.
> OSBERT SITWELL (1892–1969)
> on John Singer Sargent and his sitters
> *Left Hand, Right Hand*

When Edward Burra (1905–76) was asked by his friend, William Chappell, why he painted his figures transparent, he replied: 'Don't you find as you get older that you start seeing through people?'

Amusing. But try to suppress these things for a time; they will come out all the more strongly later. For the present you should paint labourers.
> MAX BECKMANN (1884–1950)
> advice to students who attempted over-ambitious compositions

In the midst of some abominable views of Venice, one discovers a charming portrait by M. Renoir; had he learned to draw, M. Renoir would have made a very pleasing canvas out of his 'Boating Party'.
> ALBERT WOLFF
> review in *Le Figaro* of the Exhibition of Independent artists
> 2 March, 1882

To get someone to pose, you have to be very good friends and above all speak the language.
AUGUSTE RENOIR (1841–1914)
letter to Charles Deudon
Naples, December 1881

However ugly a face may be, we can discover some beauty in it if we first experience wonder before it and then begin to understand it, too.
OSKAR KOKOSCHKA (1886–1980)
Dialogues: Conversations with European Artists at Mid-Century
Edouard Roditi
1958

A portrait, to be a work of art, neither must nor may resemble the sitter . . . the painter has within himself the landscapes he wishes to produce. To depict a figure one must not paint that figure; one must paint its atmosphere.
UMBERTO BOCCIONI (1882–1916)
Technical Manifesto of Futurist Painting
11 April, 1910

As regards the supreme reasons against the admission of the female students to the study of the male nude, they cannot be mentioned to a maiden's ears.
Seeking and Saving
February 1885

When, in 1893, women students at the Royal Academy Schools were at last allowed to draw from the nude male model, the Council stipulated that he must wear bathing drawers over which a length of material, nine feet by three feet, should be wound – and, finally, a belt on top.

I'm sick of Portraits and wish very much to take my Viol da Gamba and walk off to some sweet Village where I can paint Landskips and enjoy the fag End of Life in quietness and ease.

> THOMAS GAINSBOROUGH (1727–88)
> letter to William Jackson

I have now got a bombproof shelter [the Continent] into which I retire when I sniff the coming portrait or its trajectory.

> JOHN SINGER SARGENT (1856–1925)
> letter to his friend Lady Lewis
> 1906

In our fine arts, not imitation, but creation is the aim. In landscapes, the painter should give the suggestion of a fairer creation than we know. The details, the prose of nature, he should omit, and give us only the spirit and splendour . . . In a portrait, he must inscribe the character, and not the features, and must esteem the man who sits to him as himself only an imperfect picture or likeness of the aspiring original within.

    RALPH WALDO EMERSON (1803–82)
    Essays

Remember that a picture – before being a horse, a nude, or some sort of anecdote – is essentially a flat surface covered with colours assembled in a certain order.

    MAURICE DENIS (1870–1943)
    Art et Critique
    1890

My picture is nearly finished, it is *très loin de* Sickert. He by the way spends at least two hours daily at tea-time in holding forth. I always say yes and go home and do the opposite.

    NINA HAMNETT (1890–1956)
    letter to Roger Fry

A little amateur painting in water-colours shows the innocent and quiet mind.

    ROBERT LOUIS STEVENSON (1850–94)
    Virginibus Puerisque

A Raphael is not a painting in the National Gallery – it is an active force in our lives.

> BEN NICHOLSON (1894–1982)
> Notes on 'Abstract' Art
> *Horizon*, October 1941

Art is the objectification of feeling, and the subjectification of nature.

> SUSANNE LANGER (1895–1985)
> *Mind, An Essay on Human Feeling*

———⟨⟩———

The way to ensure summer in England is to have it framed and glazed in a comfortable room.

> HORACE WALPOLE, Fourth Earl of Orford (1717–97)
> *Letters*

Stanley Spencer (1891-1959) was often asked if he had painted in Paris. 'No,' he would reply. 'What is wrong in painting in Cookham?'

> WILLIAM ROTHENSTEIN, *Stanley Spencer*

Standing in front of Frith's 'Derby Day', Oscar Wilde (1854–1900) murmured 'Is it really all done by hand?'

You can look at a painting for a whole week and then never think about it again. You can also look at a painting for a second and think about it for the rest of your life.

JOAN MIRÓ (1893–1983)
interview with Yvon Taillandier
1959

My painting does not come from the easel . . . On the floor I am more at ease. I feel nearer, more a part of the painting, since this way I can walk around it, work from the four sides and literally be *in* the painting.

JACKSON POLLOCK (1912–56)
'My Painting', *Possibilities 1*, winter 1947–8

For me the acid test of a painting is: will the ordinary chap get anything out of this?

> CAREL WEIGHT (born 1908)
> to Linda Saunders
> *Modern Painters*: A Quarterly Journal of the Fine Arts, 1994

When the emotions are strong and one feels pent up, one should paint bamboo; in a light mood one should paint the orchid.

> CHÜEH YIN
> Buddhist monk of the Yüan period, 1279–1368
> as quoted in E. H. Gombrich, *Art and Illusion*

I do not repudiate any of my paintings but there is not one of them that I would not redo differently.

> HENRI MATISSE (1869–1954)
> *Notes of a Painter*
> 1908

Trees! How ghastly!

> PIET MONDRIAN (1872–1944)
> on being invited by Kandinsky to admire the wonderful view from his apartment in Neuilly

I am bracing my eye on Rubens and Rembrandt. Churchill.

> telegram from SIR WINSTON CHURCHILL (1874–1965) in Amsterdam to Walter Sickert

Creation will lead us out of our difficulties where materialism has failed.

ALEXANDER ARCHIPENKO (1887–1964)
The Science of Creation

Whatever else is in my paintings, I do feel that there is something of the human spirit. They're also biological. It's amazing when you look through a microscope and recognize how many shapes and forms we've grown used to seeing in abstract painting.

SANDRA BLOW (born 1925)
interview with Judith Bumpus
Royal Academy Magazine, winter 1993

What the rest of us see only under the influence of mescalin, the artist is congenitally equipped to see all the time.

ALDOUS HUXLEY (1894–1963)
The Doors of Perception

These chickens were painted by John James Audubon in one morning before one o'clock lunch, as someone visiting him told him he did not believe such rapid work could be done.

JOHN JAMES AUDUBON (1780–1851)
note affixed to a meticulous study of a rooster and hens

In painting, the gravest immorality is to try to finish what isn't well begun. But a picture that is well begun may be left off at any point. Look at Cézanne's water colours!
SIR MATTHEW SMITH (1879–1959)

I'm not an abstractionist . . . I'm not interested in relationships of colour or form or anything else.
MARK ROTHKO (1903–70)

Beauty is a paradox. Nature is a paradox. Really great art is paradoxical. It can transform ugliness into beauty. But beauty is its basis, not ugliness. Anybody who thinks he's being clever by painting an ugly picture can pack up.
VICTOR PASMORE (born 1908)
to Andrew Lambirth
The Royal Academy Magazine, winter 1993

I have learned that what I have not drawn, I have never really seen, and that when I start drawing an ordinary thing, I realize how extraordinary it is, sheer miracle.

FREDERICK FRANCK (born 1909)
The Zen of Seeing

Whenever you think you can make a drawing better, MAKE IT BETTER ON ANOTHER PIECE OF PAPER. It keeps things clearer and saves us from the worst consequences of misjudgement and the tired eye.

GORDON BOTTOMLEY (1874–1948)
letter to Paul Nash
17 May, 1912

Marcel Duchamp's famous work, 'Large Glass: The Bride Stripped Bare by Her Bachelors, Even', took twelve years to bring it to what he called a state of final incompletion. He announced that it was 'finished' only when it was accidentally cracked in 1926.

I succeeded in simply attending at the birth of all my works.

MAX ERNST (1891–1976)

Art is the imposing of a pattern on experience, and our aesthetic enjoyment is recognition of the pattern.

ALFRED NORTH WHITEHEAD (1861–1947)
Dialogues
10 June, 1943

Study the sublime dreams of Piranesi, who seems to have conceived visions of Rome beyond what it boasted even in the meridian of its splendour, savage as Salvator Rosa, fierce as Michael Angelo and exuberant as Rubens, he has imagined scenes that would startle geometry, and exhaust the Indies to realize. He piles palaces on bridges, and temples on palaces, and scales Heaven with mountains of edifices. Yet what taste in his boldness! What labour and thought both in his rashness and details!

> HORACE WALPOLE, Fourth Earl of Orford (1717–97)
> *Anecdotes of Painting in England*, Preface to vol. IV
> 1771

Manet wanted one day to paint my wife and children. Renoir was there. He took a canvas and began painting them too. After a while, Manet took me aside and whispered, 'You're on very good terms with Renoir and take an interest in his future – do advise him to give up painting! You can see for yourself that it's not his *métier* at all.'

> CLAUDE MONET (1840–1926)
> to Ambroise Vollard
> *Recollections of a Picture Dealer*

My dear Tristan, to be an artist *at all* is like living in Switzerland during a world war.

> TOM STOPPARD (born 1937)
> *Travesties*
> 1974

Drawing and colour are not separate at all; in so far as you paint, you draw. The more the colour harmonises, the more exact the drawing becomes. When the colour achieves richness, the form attains its fullness also.

> PAUL CÉZANNE (1839–1906)
> to Emile Bernard at Aix; subsequently published in the magazine *L'Occident*
> July 1904

The beautiful is that which excites the aesthetic sense in the artist. What is beautiful to an artist to-day will be beautiful to all and sundry in ten years.

> W. SOMERSET MAUGHAM (1874–1965)
> *A Writer's Notebook*
> 1896

Color is the keyboard, the eyes are the hammers, the soul is the piano with many strings. The artist is the hand that plays, touching one key or another purposively, to cause vibrations in the soul.

> WASSILY KANDINSKY (1866–1944)
> *The Art of Spiritual Harmony*: essay

All profoundly original art looks ugly at first.

> CLEMENT GREENBERG (1909–94)

This picture [Salisbury Cathedral from the Bishop's Grounds] was Painted in the year 1823 by John Constable Esq. R.A. and was given to me by my dear

Father the Bishop of Salisbury as a wedding present. At his especial request the small piece of blue sky was inserted as making it a more suitable marriage gift than the cloudy skies usual in his Pictures.

E. MIREHOUSE, July 1877
note found tucked between the canvas and the stretcher

Even an abstract form has to have a likeness.
WILLEM DE KOONING (born 1904)

When you stop doing something, it doesn't mean you are rejecting the previous work . . . it's saying I have exploited it enough now and I wish to take a look at another corner.
DAVID HOCKNEY (born 1937)
David Hockney

It is precisely from the regret left by the imperfect work that the next one can be born.
ODILON REDON (1840–1916)
To Myself

I don't very much enjoy looking at paintings in general. I
know too much about them. I take them apart.
GEORGIA O'KEEFFE (1887–1986)
Alexander Fried, 'An Artist of Her Own School';
San Francisco Examiner and Chronicle, 16 March,
1971

Anna de Smytere, the wife of the sculptor Jan de Heere and mother of Lucas de Heere 'made a picture of a windmill with every nail on the wing and a miller in it, loaded with a bag, and climbing the mill; below on the crest of the hill were a horse and wagon and people walking. This entire picture could be covered by half an ear of wheat'.

KAREL VAN MANDER (1548–1606)
The Painter's Book, 1604

Goya (1746–1828) wrote that he had three masters: Nature, Velásquez and Rembrandt.

quoted in Chabrun, *Goya* (1965)

Braque, Matisse and Cézanne, and nobody else – nobody.
NICOLAS DE STAËL (1914–55)

The only real influence I've ever had was myself.
EDWARD HOPPER (1882–1967)
Alexander Eliot, *Three Hundred Years of American Painting*

Titian might have thought Frith intolerably common but he would have recognized that he was practising the same art as himself. He could not think this of Picasso.

EVELYN WAUGH (1903–66)
letter to Robin Campbell
1945

If Picasso drips, I drip . . . For a long while I was *with* Cézanne, and now I am *with* Picasso.

>ARSHILE GORKY (1905–48)
>Dore Ashton, *American Art Since 1945*

Yet in spite of the total disregard of the dictionary of manners, he shows a politeness toward us which no other man here would have shown . . . Cézanne is one of the most liberal artists I have ever seen. He prefaces every remark with *Pour moi* it is so and so, but he grants that everyone may be as honest and as true to nature from their convictions; he doesn't believe that everyone should see alike.

>MARY CASSATT (1845–1926)
>letter to Mrs Stillman
>1894

Mary Cassatt, sister of Mr. Cassatt, president of the Pennsylvania Railroad, returned from Europe yesterday. She has been studying painting in France, and owns the smallest Pekingese dog in the world.

>*Public Ledger*, Philadelphia
>1899

Close your bodily eye, that you may see your picture first with the eye of the spirit. Then bring to light what you have seen in the darkness, that its effect may work back, from without to within.

>CASPAR DAVID FRIEDRICH (1774–1840)
>Carus, *Friedrich der Landschaftmaler* (1841)

If necessary, I would even paint with my bottom.
JEAN-HONORÉ FRAGONARD (1732–1806)
studio anecdote recorded *c.* 1850–60 by Jules
Renouvier and published after his death in *Histoire
de l'art pendant la Révolution* (1863)

When I pass Doc. Price's tattoo shop I am often tempted
to have one myself: something rather genteel I think –
like my paintings.
BERYL COOK (born 1926)
One Man Show

People say I think too much about women, yet, after all
what is there more important to think about?
AUGUSTE RODIN (1840–1917)
William Rothenstein, *Men and Memories* (1927)

One must not imitate the sun, one must make oneself
into a sun.
RAOUL DUFY (1877–1953)

I do not belong to any school; I simply want to do something that is personal to myself.
PIERRE BONNARD (1867–1947)

Painting is an essentially *concrete* art and can only consist
of the representation of *real and existing things* . . . an
object which is abstract, not visible, non-existent, is not
within the realm of painting.
GUSTAVE COURBET (1819–77)

But all categories of art, idealistic or realistic, surrealistic or constructivist (a new form of idealism) must satisfy a simple test (or they are in no sense works of art): they must persist as objects of contemplation.

SIR HERBERT READ (1893–1968)
Modern Sculpture

I have lived enough among painters and around studios to have had all the theories – and how contradictory they are – rammed down my throat. A man has to have a gizzard like an ostrich to digest all the brass-tacks and wire nails of modern art theories.

D.H. LAWRENCE (1885–1930)
Assorted Articles

Come now, Spencer, don't be so damned spiritual. Beef or mutton?

WALTER SICKERT (1860–1942)
at lunch with Stanley Spencer

Vuillard balances too far on the side of fantasy . . . The people in his pictures are not properly defined. As he's an admirable draughtsman it must be that he just *doesn't want* to give them mouths and hands and feet.

PAUL SIGNAC (1863–1935)
diary
1898

One day Courbet refused to permit the admission, to an exhibition of his pictures that he had not finished hanging, of an impatient group of quidnuncs. On second thoughts he asked, 'Who are those men?'

'Monsieur Courbet, they are members of a rifle club.'

'Then show the gentlemen in! They are people who can see straight!'

WALTER SICKERT (1860–1942)
A Free House!

Sir Edward Burne-Jones (1833-98) considered it a desecration that smoking and flirtation should take place in the presence of his canvases.

When you've responded to Goya it's impossible to take Delacroix seriously.

LAWRENCE GOWING (born 1918)

I certainly consider a great appreciation of painting to be the best indication of a most perfect mind, even though it happens that this art is pleasing to the uneducated as well as to the educated.

LEON BATTISTA ALBERTI (1404–72)
On Painting
translated by John R. Spencer

In November 1883 *Punch* printed an imaginary conversation between Whistler and Oscar Wilde on Art and Life, prompting the following exchange of telegrams:

WILDE: *Punch* too ridiculous. When you and I are together we never talk about anything but ourselves.

WHISTLER: No, no, Oscar, you forget. When you and I are together we never talk about anything except me.

WILDE: It is true Jimmy we were talking about you, but I was thinking of myself.

Painting can start with anything, provided it ends with painting. The most literary, poetic, romantic, what you will, can only be judged by this standard, and this alone.
    JOHN MINTON (1917–57)
    BBC radio broadcast
    22 May, 1947

If you ask me what the world looks like to me, it looks like a painting by Pissarro.
    PROFESSOR SIR ERNST GOMBRICH (born 1909)
    A Lifelong Interest: Conversations on Art and Science with Didier Eribon

Painting for a whole morning gives one as excellent an appetite for one's dinner, as old Abraham Tucker acquired for his by riding over Banstead Downs.
    WILLIAM HAZLITT (1778–1830)
    Table Talk

Degas is nothing but a peeping Tom, behind the *coulisses*, and among the dressing-rooms of the ballet dancers, noting only travesties of fallen debased womanhood, most disgusting and offensive.

> *The Churchman*
> May 1886

I'll always be grateful to rent collecting. I've put many of the tenants in my pictures.

> L.S. LOWRY (1887–1976)

Copy the works of the Almighty first and those of Turner next.

> EDWARD LEAR (1812–88)
> advice to a student

The only difference between an artist and a lunatic is, perhaps, that the artist has the restraint or courtesy . . . to conceal the intensity of his obsession from all except those similarly afflicted.

> OSBERT SITWELL (1892–1969)
> *A Short Character of Walter Richard Sickert*
> introduction to *A Free House!* by Walter Richard Sickert

It was said that in the company of Degas even James McNeill Whistler's conversation was reduced to 'brilliant flashes of silence'.

Energy is eternal delight; and from the earliest times human beings have tried to imprison it in some durable hieroglyphic. It is perhaps the first of all the subjects of art.

LORD CLARK (1903–83)
The Nude: A Study of Ideal Art

Boredom soon overcomes me when I am contemplating nature.

EDGAR DEGAS (1834-1917)
Notebook, 1858

The *sans-gêne* and promptitude with which many painters, on arriving at an entirely new and unfamiliar place, settle down to work at once, never fails to astonish me: it seems indecent, like button-holing a complete stranger.

AUGUSTUS JOHN (1878–1961)
Chiaroscuro

Alas, the very name of *picture* produces a sadness of heart I cannot describe. Painting has been a smiling mistress to many, but she has been a cruel jilt to me; I did not abandon her, she abandoned me. I have no wish to be remembered as a painter, for I never was a painter; my idea of that profession *was* perhaps too exalted; I may say, *is* too exalted. I leave it to others more worthy to fill the niches of art.

SAMUEL MORSE (1791–1872)
letter to James Fenimore Cooper

Art completes what nature cannot bring to a finish.
ARISTOTLE (384–322 BC)

If today's arts love the machine, technology and organization, if they aspire to precision and reject anything vague and dreamy, this implies an instinctive repudiation of Chaos and a longing to find the form appropriate to our times.
OSKAR SCHLEMMER (1888–1943)
diary, April 1926

Painting a picture is not a form of self-expression. It is, like any other art, a language by which you communicate something about the world.
MARK ROTHKO (1903–70)
lecture delivered at Pratt Institute in 1958

A painter was asked why, since he made such beautiful figures, which were but dead things, his children were so ugly; to which the painter replied that he made his pictures by day, and his children by night.
LEONARDO DA VINCI (1452–1519)
Literary Works

Human beings in Chinese art are no longer specimens of *homo sapiens*. They are examples of *homo aestheticus*. In their rarefied presence I begin to long for Courbet's giggling, sweating wenches.
ERIC NEWTON (1893–1965)
European Painting and Sculpture

Nothing as drastic an innovation as abstract art could have come into existence, save as the consequence of a most profound, relentless, unquenchable need. The need is for felt experience – intense, immediate, direct, subtle, unified, warm, vivid, rhythmic.

ROBERT MOTHERWELL (born 1915)
What Abstract Art Means to Me
The Museum of Modern Art Bulletin, spring 1951

I incorporate visual data that is liable to come from any time or place . . . One ends up with a landscape one has never seen before but it is presumably the landscape you were feeling as you started the painting.

SIR SIDNEY NOLAN (born 1917)

Outside is the world; it's there. Pop art looks out into the world.

ROY LICHTENSTEIN (born 1928)

There be more things to greet the heart and eyes
In Arno's dome of Art's most princely shrine,
Where Sculpture with her rainbow sister vies;
There be more marvels yet – but not for mine;
For I have been accustom'd to entwine
My thoughts with Nature rather in the fields,
Than Art in galleries.

LORD BYRON (1788–1824)
Childe Harold's Pilgrimage

The time of year when the devil comes and spews art over London.

JOHN CONSTABLE (1776–1837)
on the Royal Academy's Summer Exhibition

Well, something must be done for May.
     The time is drawing nigh –
To figure in the Catalogue,
     And woo the public eye.
Something I must invent and paint;
     But oh my wit is not
Like one of those kind substantives
     That answer Who and What?
     THOMAS HOOD (1799–1845)
     The Painter Puzzled

Varnishing is the only artistic process with which Royal Academicians are thoroughly familiar.
OSCAR WILDE (1854–1900)

Our Exhibitions [The Royal Academy] have also a mischievous tendency, by seducing the Painter to an ambition of pleasing indiscriminately the mixed multitude of people who resort to them.
SIR JOSHUA REYNOLDS (1723–92)
Discourses

The works of art, by being publicly exhibited and offered for sale, are becoming articles of trade, following as such the unreasoning laws of markets and fashion; and public and even private patronage is swayed by their tyrannical influence.
ALBERT, PRINCE CONSORT (1819–61)
speech at the Royal Academy Dinner
3 May, 1851

'The best way to begin,' said Balthazar Balthus, having insisted that the catalogue for his 1968 exhibition at the Tate Gallery should contain no biographical matter, 'is to say: Balthus is a painter of whom *nothing is known*. And now let us have a look at his paintings.'

Every painting I do is related to the last one: it may be a continuation of a previous painting or it may be a re-action against it. When I grow tired of grey I long for colour so I use colour.
WILLIAM SCOTT (born 1913)
Lawrence Alloway, *Nine Abstract Artists*
1954

The beautiful is that which is desirable *in itself*.
ARISTOTLE (384–322 BC)

Taste is the death of a painter.
WALTER SICKERT (1860–1942)
A Free House!

The French have taste in all they do,
Which we are quite without;
For Nature, which to them gave *goût*
To us gave only gout.

Art will never be able to exist without nature.
PIERRE BONNARD (1867–1947)

She [the artist's wife] will know that there is no more sombre enemy of good art than the pram in the hall.
CYRIL CONNOLLY (1903–74)
The Charlock's Shade

I am a child who is getting on.
>   MARC CHAGALL (1887–1985)
>   towards the end of his life

Chagall is my favourite pupil, and what I like about him is that after listening attentively to my lessons he takes his paints and brushes and does something absolutely different from what I have told him.
>   LEON BAKST (1866–1924)

Artists may produce excellent designs, but they will avail little, unless the taste of the public is sufficiently cultivated to appreciate them.
>   GEORGE C. MASON
>   *Art Manufactures*

The reality of life is incomprehensible, and the Artist creates an incomprehensible image of it.
>   CECIL COLLINS (born 1908)
>   Tate Gallery exhibition catalogue
>   1989

One cannot explain the existence of genius. It is better to enjoy it.
>   PROFESSOR SIR ERNST GOMBRICH (born 1909)
>   *The Story of Art*

'Genius?', I remember an aunt saying to my mother about a clever little cousin, 'nonsense, dear, he's as strong as a horse.'

> SIR HUGH CASSON (born 1910)
> *Diary*

It takes a lot of time to be a genius, you have to sit around so much doing nothing really doing nothing.

> GERTRUDE STEIN (1874–1946)
> *Everybody's Autobiography*, 1937

Men of genius sometimes accomplish most when they work the least, for they are thinking out inventions and forming in their minds the perfect idea that they subsequently express with their hands.

> attributed by Giorgio Vasari to LEONARDO DA VINCI
> (1452–1519)

It is difficult to judge one's contemporaries; perhaps it is impossible to understand them.

> ODILON REDON (1840–1916)
> *To Myself*: Journal

Once you had to be a genius to make works of art. Now you have to be a genius to understand them.

> ROY EMMINS (born 1939)

Genius only comes to those who know how to use their eyes and their intelligence.

AUGUSTE RODIN (1840–1917)

For make no mistake about it, work for an artist is a highly conscious, rational process at the end of which the work of art emerges as mastered reality – not at all a state of intoxicated inspiration.

ERNST FISCHER
The Necessity of Art: A Marxist Approach

The temple of art is built of words. Painting and sculpture and music are but the blazon of its windows, borrowing all their significance from the light, and suggestive only of the temple's uses.

> J.G. HOLLAND (1819–81)
> *Plain Talks on Familiar Subjects*

After painting comes Sculpture, a very noble art, but one that does not in the execution require the same supreme ingenuity as the art of painting, since in two most important and difficult particulars, in foreshortening and in light and shade, for which the painter has to invent a process, sculpture is helped by nature. Moreover, Sculpture does not imitate colour which the painter takes pains to attune so that the shadows accompany the lights.

> LEONARDO DA VINCI (1452–1519)
> *Literary Works*

I express myself in sculpture since I am not a poet.

> ARISTIDE MAILLOL (1861–1944)
> Waldemar George, *Maillol*

As picture teaches the colouring, so sculpture the anatomy of form. When I have seen fine statues, and afterwards enter a public assembly, I understand well what he meant who said, 'When I have been reading Homer, all men look like giants'.

> RALPH WALDO EMERSON (1803–82)
> *Essays*

I say that the art of sculpture is eight times as great as any other art based on drawing, because a statue has eight views and they must all be equally good.

BENVENUTO CELLINI (1500–71)
letter to Benedetto Varchi
28 January, 1547

To be a sculptor you need to be one part artist and nine parts navvy.
JOHN SKEAPING (1901–80)

The transformation of the experience: that is pure art.
REBECCA HORN (born 1944)
interview with Anne de Charmant
Tate: The Art Magazine, winter 1994

The stone unhewn and cold
Becomes a living mould,
The more the marble wastes
The more the statue grows.
MICHELANGELO BUONARROTI (1475–1564)
Sonnet (trans. Mrs Henry Roscoe)

Exaggeration and modification are the undisputed prerogative of the creative artist.
CHARLES SARGEANT JAGGER (1885–1934)

He who perforates the stone destroys the plastic impression that dwells in it. A hole in the block of a piece of sculpture is in most cases nothing but the expression of impotence and weakness.
FRITZ WOTRUBA (1907–75)
from his private notebooks; Neuchatel, 1961

The first hole made through a piece of stone is a revelation. A piece of sculpture can have a hole through it and not be weakened – if the hole is of a studied size, shape, and direction.

HENRY MOORE (1898–1986)
'Notes on Sculpture'

In 'Pierced Form' I had felt the most intense pleasure in piercing the stone in order to make an abstract form and space; quite a different sensation from that of doing it for the purpose of realism.

BARBARA HEPWORTH (1903–75)
Barbara Hepworth: Carvings & Drawings, 1952

The art of sculpture is long ago perished to any real effect. It was originally an useful art, a mode of writing, a savage's record of gratitude or devotion; and among a people possessed of a wonderful perception of form, this childish carving was refined to the utmost splendour of effect. But it is the game of a rude and youthful people, and not the manly labour of a wise and spiritual nation.

RALPH WALDO EMERSON (1803–82)
Essays: Art

The conditions you need to be a good goalkeeper are exactly the same conditions you need to be a good sculptor! You must have a very good connection, in both professions, with time and space.

EDUARDO CHILLIDA (born 1924)
Hayward Gallery catalogue, 1990

To think of abstraction as an end in itself is undoubtedly letting oneself be led into a cul-de-sac and can only lead to exhaustion and impotence.

SIR JACOB EPSTEIN (1880–1959)
Epstein: an Autobiography
1955

They are a form of statuary which no careful father would wish his daughter, or no discriminating young man, his fiancée to see . . . For a certain type of mind, on the other hand, it cannot but have a demoralizing tendency.

FATHER BERNARD VAUGHAN
on Jacob Epstein's Strand Statues
Evening Standard, 1908

There once was a sculptor of mark,
Who was chosen to brighten Hyde Park;
  Some thought his design
  Most uncommonly fine,
But more like it best in the dark.

Punch
on Jacob Epstein's 'Rima'
1925

If you want to change your art, change your habits.

CLEMENT GREENBERG (1909–94)
to Anthony Caro
1959

I think that the image my work invokes is the image of good – not of evil; the image of order – not of chaos; the image of life – not death.   And that is all the content of my constructions amounts to.

> NAUM GABO (1890–1977)
> letter to Sir Herbert Read
> 1944

It is weight that gives meaning to weightlessness . . . I realized that lightness added to lightness does not add tension but diminishes it.

> ISAMU NOGUCHI (born 1904)
> *Sculptor's World*

For Arp, Art is Arp.

> MARCEL DUCHAMP (1887–1968)
> catalogue, *Arp*, Galleria Schwarz, Milan, 1965

Each work has its own space, which should neither be conceived as a sort of cage nor regarded as extending to infinity.

> MARINO MARINI (1901–80)

All works of nature created by God in heaven and on earth are works of sculpture.

> BENVENUTO CELLINI (1500–71)
> *Il Trattato dell' Oreficeria e della Scultura*, ed. Carlo Milanesi

My aim is for ripeness of form. I want to make my forms so full, so juicy that one could add nothing more to them.

> HENRI LAURENS (1885–1954)
> article by Y. Taillandier in *Amis de l'Art*, No. 1
> 26 June, 1951

I have read that the ancients, when they had produced a sound, used to modulate it, heightening and lowering its pitch without departing from the rules of harmony. So must the artist do in working at the nude.

> ANTONIO CANOVA (1757–1822)
> letter to Count Leopoldo Cicognara
> Rome, February 1815

Skill and technique are only means to an end, and where the end is unimportant, so are the means.

> ANNA MAHLER (born 1904)
> 'The Human Figure in Art': lecture to the
> University of Chicago
> 1962

Art is techniques (e.g. watercolour). Techniques are so mystical: if I wanted to understand an electric motor I would go to a fortune-teller.

> JEAN TINGUELY (born 1925)
> *National-Zeitung*, Basle
> 13 October, 1967

I like tense, sinewy, dry things, olive trees dried up by the wind, brittle wood . . . I am more moved by a charred tree stump than by an apple tree in flower.
> GERMAINE RICHIER (1904–59)

In art, one does not aim for simplicity; one achieves it unintentionally as one gets closer to the real meaning of things.
> CONSTANTIN BRANCUSI (1876–1957)
> catalogue, Wildenstein Galleries
> New York, 1926

My drawings are the result of my sculpture.
> AUGUSTE RODIN (1840–1917)
> a letter to Emile Antoine Bourdelle referring to his later drawings
> 1903

Where the material ends, art begins.
> ÉTIENNE HAJDU (born 1907)
> Guiseppe Marchiori, *Modern French Sculpture*

The essence of a sculpture must enter on tip-toe, as light as animal footprints on snow.
> HANS ARP (1887–1966)
> *Unsern täglichen Traum*, Zurich, 1955

To describe and explain my ideas is to lose them.
> MARINO MARINI (1901–80)
> quoted in *Marino Marini*; A. Zwemmer Ltd

When an artist explains what he is doing he usually has to do one of two things: either scrap what he has explained, or make his subsequent work fit in with the explanation.

> ALEXANDER CALDER (born 1898)
> 'Alexander Calder Mobiles' ed. Myfanwy Evans
> *The Painter's Object*, 1937

A steady iron-hard jet of absolutely total nonsense.

> WILLIAM EMPSON (1906–84)
> on the introductory copy that prefaces exhibition catalogues

Criticism is a study by which men grow important and formidable at a very small expense. The power of invention has been conferred by Nature upon few, and the labour of learning those sciences which may by mere labour be obtained is too great to be willingly endured; but every man can exert such judgment as he has upon the works of others; and he whom Nature has made weak, and Idleness keeps ignorant, may yet support his vanity by the name of a Critic.

> SAMUEL JOHNSON (1709–84)
> *Dick Minim the Critic*

There is a certain arrogance about all criticism which parallels the arrogance of the artist in setting himself up as a creator in the first place.

> EDWARD LUCIE-SMITH (born 1933)
> *Thinking About Art*

I'd much rather be liked by the people than by critics.
Much better.

BERNARD BUFFET (born 1928)
interview with Douglas Maxwell; *Modern Painters:*
A Quarterly Journal of the Fine Arts.

Art criticism everywhere is now at a low ebb, intellectu-
ally corrupt, swamped in meaningless jargon, distorted by
political correctitudes, anxiously addressed only to other
critics and their ilk.

    BRIAN SEWELL
    Evening Standard
    10 November 1994

The true work of a critic is not to make his hearer believe him, but agree with him.
JOHN RUSKIN (1819–1900)

The mere blundering of clever peasants.
JOHN RUSKIN (1819–1900)
on the work of David Cox and John Constable
Lectures on Landscape

When I was an undergraduate in the early 1960s, I was asked to understand that an interest in Ruskin was as foolish as an enthusiasm for modern art.
TIM HILTON (born 1941)
John Ruskin: The Early Years

Painting: The Art of protecting flat surfaces from the weather and exposing them to the critic.
AMBROSE BIERCE (1842–1914?)
The Enlarged Devil's Dictionary

Never to go overboard for an unknown artist is a sign of bad character in a critic.
JOHN RUSSELL (born 1919)
Private View
Robertson/Russell/Snowdon

The cynicism of the young about society is as nothing to the cynicism of young artists for the art establishment.
NANCY HALE
Mary Cassatt: A Biography of the Great American Painter, 1975

It is fatal for art if it is forced into official respectability and condemned to sterile mediocrity.
GUSTAVE COURBET (1819–77)

The man who arrives at the doors of artistic creation with none of the madness of the Muses, would be convinced that technical ability alone was enough to make an artist . . . what that man creates by means of reason will pale before the art of inspired beings.
PLATO (c. 428/7 – 348/7 BC)
Phaedrus

Abstract art, properly defined, is 'drawn from' nature, an abstract of nature . . . It could thus be made to apply to all that large field of art which lies between the non-representational and the naturalistic – a field which includes almost all African art.

> WILLIAM FAGG and MARGARET PLASS
> *African Sculpture: An Anthology*
> 1964

There is no need to express art in terms of nature. It can perfectly well be expressed in terms of geometry and the exact sciences.

> GEORGES VANTONGERLOO (1866–1965)
> *Paintings, Sculptures, Reflections; 1948*

The sole purpose of the arts is neither description nor imitation, but the creation of unknown beings from elements which are always present but not apparent.

> RAYMOND DUCHAMP–VILLON (1876–1918)
> George Heard Hamilton and William Agee,
> *Raymond Duchamp–Villon, 1967*

The immortality of great art seems bound up with the inevitable loss of its original surface meaning and its rebirth in the spirit of every new age.

> ANTON EHRENZWEIG (1908–66)
> *The Hidden Order of Art, 1967*

For the outer sense alone perceives visible things and the eye of the heart alone sees the invisible.
RICHARD OF SAINT-VICTOR (died 1173)

True story: The Major of some Lancashire town being presented with a pair of statues for the Town Hall remarked after inspecting the nude figures: 'Art is art, and nothing can be done to prevent it. But there is the Mayoress's decency to be considered!'
JAMES AGATE (1877–1947)
Ego

It is through . . . Art and Art only that we can shield ourselves from the sordid perils of actual existence.
OSCAR WILDE (1854–1900)

There really is no such thing as Art. There are only artists.
PROFESSOR SIR ERNST GOMBRICH (born 1909)
The Story of Art